Indulge

SHANNON TEDESCHI

Presentation by *BookLeaf Publishing*

Web: www.bookleafpub.com

E-mail: info@bookleafpub.com

ISBN: 9789357744300

First edition 2023

I would like to dedicate this book to some very inspirational people in my life. My son John and all of his new beginnings, my daughter Sarah who encouraged me to publish my work and who also showed me what true fearlessness looks like, my entire family and closest friends for all of their support and encouragement. Lastly, I would like to dedicate this book to a very special friend who opened my eyes without saying a word.

ACKNOWLEDGEMENT

I would like to thank all of my English teachers throughout my entire academic career. Each inspired me in their own unique way, allowing me to explore the furthest regions of my imagination and put them on paper I also want to extend a sincere "Thank you" to every stranger I've encountered over the years. Each has taught me lessons or has been a blessing and never was viewed a stranger again. I see and appreciate you.

PREFACE

The deeper the water, the tougher the pain. The brighter the sunshine, the lighter the rain.

The First Time I Saw Myself

An ordinary day, sunshine and crisp Fall air
I am comfortable yet unknowing
Destiny was impending and imminent
Eyes locking at first glance
You look familiar, have we met before?
One unexpected glance is all it took
One powerful enough to pierce even the oldest
of souls as if was new
It's me. A mentor. A warrior. A special friend
Words never spoken but known in the heart
A powerful journey is about to commence.
Ready or not...

The Beginning

Memories of familiar feelings catch the interest
Flashes of the future so blinding, hold the
interest
Now begins the game
Cast iron fences display visual strength
Change perspectives
A strong fence which also has vulnerability
Things which cannot be seen with the eyes
Time and space have conjoined and derived a
sacred plan
An unspoken agreement exists and waits
Are you coming?

Moonlight

Moonlight glistening in a light blanket of fluffy
snow
Diamonds in the cold that hold answers to both
the past and the future
At night, I come alive. When the rest of the
world is quietly asleep,
That's when I live. That's when I'm comfortable.
In shadows, deep inside my emotions
Serious. Contemplative. Strategic. Always
striving towards my goals of happiness

Chilly Nights

Fireplace and movies
Big fluffy pillows and big cozy blankets
Being sung to sleep by the pattering of the
freezing rain against the window
Falling helplessly asleep on your chest but later I
move away
Is this really happening? Is this what I want? Is
he who I want?
I silently chuckled to myself knowing full well
this is the dream that I've always wanted
I move back towards you and wrap myself up in
your arms again. Watching you sleep.
You're perfection.
You're comfort.
You're home.

The Journey

5

This Journey is not for the faint of heart
It lifts you up, then tears you apart
It gives you the intensity of a million infernos
Then leaves you wondering if he even really
knows
The love and passion I hold inside are becoming
more difficult to suppress, I no longer want to
hide
These feelings of sweet ecstasy
"Come to me now" is my nightly plea I wake
every morning you are nowhere in sight
I'm blinded by the Sun and the assurance of light
Make this fear, pain and anguish cease
Bring me love, romance, loyalty and peace
Welcome to the Journey

At Last

A song I vaguely recognize
Brings me back to a time I vowed to memorize
You appear to me out of the blue Presenting
yourself different, changed and new
This is who I saw you to be Someone who was
special and loving like me
You stand before me heart in hand Praying for a
miracle,
You slowly present a band
A band which symbolizes your undying love for
me
Bravely and heroically, you get on one knee
Although I knew who you could come back to
be
I was taken aback by your genuine chivalry
The passion between us was off the charts
Finally proclaiming to each other what was in
our hearts
That first kiss I've been dying to taste
Made me want more, I grabbed your waist
We fell into each other there was no suspense
Finally what we've been waiting for was about
to commence
There is no stopping this kind of love

This kind of love is only from above The
deepest kind you find embedded in your soul
The kind that makes you feel complete and
doesn't take a toll
The kind so powerful it transcends time and
space
We both come to climax, collapse and embrace
True love is beautiful and worth waiting for
Now we will have each other to love, cherish
and adore
At last

You

Eyes that are brown but reflect the Sun
A mind so strong, yet built to run
A vibe that speaks a million words but a voice
that speaks nothing at all
Will we ever dance together or will we let this
fall?
A devilish smile decorates your face and
intensity like this I could never replace
Arms so comfortable if only for a moment
My body yearns for more
This is utter torment
Hair as dark as a New Moon night Please take
me now there won't be a fight
How can I contain this unbridled desire?
How you do is a trait I admire

Compromise

No more games, confusion, pain or fear
We need to be together and you should be here
Let's meet in the middle because can't you see?
A love like this was destined to be

Silence

The silence between us breaks my heart
Because deep down I know we shouldn't be
apart
Not with a love like this to share
No other love could ever compare Speak to me,
not just through lyrics and signs but with words
of love that could only be the Divine's
I patiently wait for that day to arrive When the
silence is broken and I can reveal what's inside
Until then I'll hold on to what I feel
Praying to heaven this love is real

Fantasy

Is this real or fantasy?
The feeling that we were meant to be
Will I have to move on and grow to love
another?
Continue to keep my attraction undercover?
Love you from afar, just meeting in dreams?
Consciously silencing the internal screams
You drive me mad but make me sane
After meeting you, love doesn't mean the same

Start Again

Compelled by your spirit entranced by your gaze
I know in my heart this is more than a phase
A core belief that there is something more
Something intriguing, something I long to
explore
Bring me your hardships, your struggles, your
pain
I'll make you feel new, like you've been cleansed
by the rain
Let's start again, let the heart take the lead
The lack of expression is what made our hearts
bleed

A Forehead Kiss

A forehead kiss is what I bestowed on you
To assist you with awakening, so you could see
what was true
Open your mind, your heart and your soul
Allow me to enter and lose control Let's get
wild, crazy and explore
For this is a love that is meant to endure
Trust yourself and me as well Because a life
without you has been pure hell
One sweet kiss on your forehead as you sleep
A small gesture to prove this love you can keep

Star Band

14

On any other clear, winter night a bazillion stars
would be seen
But not tonight
Tonight was a different kind of winter night sky
Tonight, a single band of stars lit up the sky in a
way never observed before
A star band if you will
A formation of stars coming together to form a
cosmic boomerang
One that announced your return home to me
Welcoming you home before a single foot
crossed the threshold of my door and heart

See Through My Eyes

15

See life through my eyes see things from my
perspective I never wanted you to save me I
wanted your presence while I saved myself
A big feet indeed to ask while someone is busy
saving themselves, Maybe my mere presence
would have given you the same comfort I sought
from you
But before a journey of two can start, a solo
journey needs to end For the both of us
My wish is that you see things through my eyes
Maybe then, you will truly understand and see
what a reflection can do and truly be

Reality

What is reality?
Is it what we see?
Is it what we feel?
Is it what we think or believe?
Could reality be just a dream that we ground?
Or is it everything combined to make our
nighttime Liaisons come true?
It all starts with a spark of inspiration from a
wild and vivid imagination
The best friend to a dream and a cousin or close
sibling to reality
It brings that creative spark that Ignites a future
vision
Do things differently, see things from a bigger
perspective
Then and only then will you reap your rewards

Glistening Snow

17

A dream that was dreamed so long ago
So vivid, so real, so quiet and peaceful
Under the rays of a glorious full moon
A blanket of glistening white snow covers the
darkness
Sparkling like diamonds that only I can see
But why?
It feels like it's a shared vision, even if I am the
sole witness of such beautiful tranquility
A feeling this beautiful must mean there is love
Even if it has yet to bless these lips

Look Through

Eyes gentle enough to break through to even the
most dark and confused soul
You know me, or better yet I know you
Maybe not from this lifetime, maybe from a
previous one
Your gaze makes me blush, shying away from
who I really am
You see it don't you?
You know this is real
Can you see the light?
Can't you feel the warmth?
Can't you feel the pain?
Just look through
You will know undoubtedly we were meant to
be
We are the same

High Sign

Beautiful Hawks follow me throughout each
waking day Numbers configure to symbolic
meanings
Haunted by past efforts, how did it go so wrong?
It was feeling so right Am I mad? Is this all in
my head? Flying above, I get my answers Those
calls that ring in my ears
The beauty that blinds my sight that is them
I trust in whatever is unfolding is meant to in
this way
I pray for the strength to deal with a devastating
heartbreak
My heart crashes to the floor once again
You appear blind to my pain,
But my beautiful sky birds have been gifted with
crystal clear vision They protect me, blessing me
with their presence

When Is It My Time?

I feel like I've been waiting forever When is it
my time?
I've watched others grow, blossom and glow in
love's pure white light
When is it my time?
Patience can't last forever
I feel like I'm doing myself a disservice waiting
on my love
When is it my time?
Giving up has never been an option This may
have to be a first
When is it my time?
I'm ready but that may not be the case for you
I'm hurting myself holding on
When is it my time?
Slowly I fade away
Now is my time

The Mask

A mask, one that covers the soul
Hiding away the face of a once true love
It brings chaos and confusion
To the most pure of hearts
True motives that are tucked away
Far away from the rest of the world to see
I want to be your shelter
I want to be your home
A safe place you can run to when you feel all
alone
This endless game of Hide and Seek
Tires the weary heart, shatters the confidence of
one brave soul
Erases evidence of a once-perceived love story
In order to truly love, one needs to let it fall
Forever isn't promised, but neither is today
So let your mask fall so you can truly live

The Longest Goodbye

Goodbye is never easy
You've lived in my heart for so long
Owning that space, but never staying there
Others have entered but never compared to you
Vowing to stay and be a part of this life I built
I decline, recoiling into myself and hiding away
It's not enough for me
Neither are you now
What, if anything, will make this easier?
Nothing.
This is my longest goodbye

ABOUT THE AUTHOR

Shannon obtained a Bachelor of Science degree in Behavioral Psychology from Northeastern University. She's the proud mother of two children ages 20 and 13. She has been working in the Human Services field for over 25 years. Shannon resides in Rockland, Massachusetts with her daughter Sarah and cat, Merlin. She has always had a passion for writing and enjoys being able to paint pictures with words.